Loving Who You Are

Loving Who You Are

A Self-Care Guide To
Nurture Your Body, Spirit, Mind

Dena Leigh Carter

Loving Who You Are, A Self-Care Guide To Nurture Your Body, Spirit, Mind. Copyright© 2015 by Dena Leigh Carter, all rights reserved. No part of this book may be used or reproduced in any manner without written permission except in the case of brief quotations in critical articles and reviews.

Contact author for permission: solehealing@denacarter.com or denaleighcarter.com

The author of this book does not dispense medical advice or prescribe the use of any technique as a form of treatment for physical, emotional, or medical problems without the advice of a physician, either directly or indirectly. The intent of the author is only to offer information of a general nature to help you in your quest for emotional and spiritual wellbeing. In the event you use any of the information in this book for yourself, the author and the publisher assume no responsibility for your actions.

ISBN 978-0-692-19316-7

All illustrations and quotes by Dena Leigh Carter with the exception of one quote: "move your body and you move your mind," by Gurmukh Kaur Khalsa. Cover and back page layout by Sunshine Design.

Additional copies of *Loving Who You Are*, *A Self-Care Guide To Nurture Your Body, Spirit, Mind,* may be purchased at booksellers or online.

Through the courage of self-expression and the love of self-care, we can come to know who we are - our true selves.

CONTENTS

A Personal Introduction	ix
About Self Care	1
What Is Self-Care?	4
The Benefits of Self Care	6
How Do I Begin Self-Care?	9
Tuning In To Your Spirit	13
Honoring and Loving Your Body	17
Honoring and Loving Your Inner Body	20
Honoring and Loving Your Outer Body	23
Moving and Praising Your Body	25
Expressing Your Creativity	28
Nurturing Yourself	31
Balancing and Harmonizing Your Mind	36
Self-Care and The Self-Love Connection	39
Abundance: A Self-Care Poem	45
Self-Care Is	47
A Message For You	49
Acknowledgements	50

A Personal Introduction

I remember a time when self-care was not a part of my life. For nearly fifteen years, I experienced chronic anxiety, depression and panic. Low self-esteem, unresolved emotional pain, poor nutrition and unhealthy personal relationships had become a way of life for me.

After experiencing an emotional breakdown in my early thirties, I knew I had to do something different. I needed to change. I left city life, my boyfriend, and my career and moved to the country. To my surprise, I discovered that moving and leaving my surroundings wasn't the sole answer.

More than outer change, I needed real inner change. I needed to slow down, connect with myself and feel my spirit. I needed to spend more time in nature and get back "down to earth." I needed to listen to my inner voice and heal my body, spirit and mind.

I began to learn a new way of life and being in the world. I simplified and got down to basics. I discovered how to make inner changes through body-spirit-mind education. The alternative healing therapies, herbal medicines, classes, books and people that helped shift my perspective and my life, all supported one important concept: self-care.

With consistent self-care, a healthy pattern began to emerge in my life and I began to heal. I learned that making significant and sustainable change wasn't about saving the world but about saving myself.

The most rewarding and unexpected part of my commitment to self-care was the discovery of self-love. Through self-care, I uncovered that much of my suffering came as a result of not knowing how to love myself.

Fifteen years later, I still practice self-care everyday.

Using the tools in this book, my wish is that you, too, feel the connectivity and empowerment self-care can bring and how it can open a gateway to self-love and healing.

Loving Who You Are

About Self-Care

We are taught many things during childhood and throughout our adolescent and adult life. But one thing we haven't been taught much about is self-care - the basic foundation and fundamentals of knowing how to care for oneself emotionally, physically, mentally and spiritually.

Self-care is something you can do right now. No matter where you are, whether at home, school, work, by yourself or in relationship. No matter what you have been through or are going through- female or male, young or old, you can begin self-care now.

With an overload of television programming, internet information, social media, entertainment and news, we become distracted from connecting with our own authentic spirit. Tuning in to self-care and actualizing it in our daily lives will create strength, balance and peace of mind.

Self-care is not a one-time thing. It is a lifelong relationship you establish - with yourself.

What Is Self-Care?

Self-care starts with *accepting yourself* as you are now and doing what you need to do to value, honor and care for yourself. Self-care is about cultivating self-awareness and merges all aspects of your being.

Whether you are sitting in silence or talking with a friend, the various choices you make in maintaining self-care are ever changing. Sometimes, it means relying on yourself, and other times it means asking for help. Whatever it is, the beauty of self-care is the self being aware of what it truly needs, *without judgment*.

With self-care, you can create a foundation to build upon in order to grow healthier, happier and more beautiful - inside and out.

The Benefits of Self-Care

Learning self-care helps you deal with some of life's significant issues: anxiety, change, stress, personal relationships, physical and mental health. Self-care is equally important to remember during times of happiness and excitement in order to keep your flow and balance.

Practicing self-care will help you get to know yourself. The more you know yourself, the more self-trust you will gain. Having self-trust is like having your own 'support system' built within you. It can give you the confidence to know when and how to nurture your well-being.

Like a vehicle, if you ignore self-care, your life will have complications or even break down. When you maintain and become aware of yourself, even in small ways, you just might have a smooth running machine for a long time. Take pride, preserve and value yourself - you are the only YOU you've got.

Ultimately *you* are the one who makes the choice to connect with your body, spirit and mind.

How Do I Begin Self-Care, What Would it Look Like?

Naturally, self-care is different for everyone, but a basic place to start is by checking in with yourself. A simple 3-step process that I do is this one:

3 Things You Can Do To Check in With Yourself

1. Take 3 minutes to slow down, stop what you are doing and BREATHE. If possible, close your eyes. Become aware of your breath. Slowly inhale through the nose and slowly exhale out the mouth. Relax your face. If your mind wanders, slow it down by

coming back to the slow inhale and exhale of your breath.

2. Place one hand on your heart and the other hand on your belly. Listen to yourself, to your body and feelings. Inhale slowly for 3 counts, pause for one count, and then exhale for 3 counts, this time through the nose and out the nose. Feel your hands on your heart and belly and relax. Listen and breathe. Do this for three minutes.

3. Next, ask yourself, what do you need? What would be the most caring and loving step you could take for yourself right now? Do you need to slow down or rest? Move the body by walking or exercising? Have some body-work done? Time to eat healthy or get a treat? Time for silence or to call someone? Get your work done or take a break? Do you need to say no or yes? Do you need to talk with someone and express how you feel? Do you need to accept or

> forgive something within yourself? Perhaps you simply need to slow down, breathe, and just 'be.'

When I am stressed or overwhelmed - physically, emotionally or mentally - I've learned to lie down and do something gentle and light. I don't push. I stretch my body out onto the floor and listen to beautiful music. I have a massage, read a book or do gentle yoga. I cancel an engagement and cook a healthy meal, call a friend or take a walk. If I feel run down or sick, I take a bath or herbal medicine, sleep or see a health practitioner. When I'm tired, I make sure not to compound things by staying up late, taking on more work and saying yes to social invitations.

Silence is a passageway to quieting the mind. Quiet the mind and hear your spirit.

Tuning In To Your Spirit

Inhaling and exhaling your breath slowly and fully, helps quiet the mind and aligns you with your spirit, your 'center.' Conscious breathing helps cultivate the stillness and calm you need to *listen* and tune in to *you*.

Through your own thoughts and feelings you can learn about yourself. By tuning in to your body sensations during time spent at work, with friends, family, and lovers, you become aware of what your needs are - your boundaries, your likes and dislikes. Learning to discover how *you are feeling* regardless of what other people feel or want for you is powerful self-care.

Self-care requires time alone so you can process your emotions and thoughts, contemplate and reflect without interference from computers, cell phones or other people. Time alone also gives you an opportunity to rely on yourself, listen to your intuition and understand the *essence* of your own spirit.

Learning to meditate will enhance your self-care and increase your capacity for silence and stillness. Meditation connects you with your breath and intuition and does wonders for keeping anxiety at bay. Yogi masters say that some form of daily meditation is crucial for bringing peace of mind, especially during challenging times.

A simple tuning in and relaxation-meditation technique:

Lay down on the ground on your back. Eyes can be open or closed. Bend your knees and place the bottoms of your feet flat on the floor. Stretch your arms out along your sides, with palms open toward the sky. Relax your shoulders and your face. Begin with a few full deep breaths and then allow your breath to flow naturally, as you inhale and exhale through the nose and out the nose. Give yourself all the time you need to relax your entire body, starting with at least five minutes. Focus only on the natural inhale and exhale of your breath. Feel your belly rise and fall. Allow your thoughts to come and go as you breathe. As your body relaxes, feel it melt into the earth.

Authentic beauty and confidence awaken when you honor and accept your unique body style.

Honoring and Loving Your Body

The body is a temple, a sacred place to call home. It is also a vehicle for greater love and connection. Beyond how your body looks on the outside, it has the potential to enhance your understanding of your inner gifts. No matter what size, shape or color, honor and love your body for its unique beauty - seen and unseen.

Be kind to yourself. Focus on the attributes and strengths of your body type. Recognize that it can help empower and serve you in your life, rather than weaken you.

Affirm positive beliefs about your body, even if you wish it to be or look different. Feel into your heart and listen to the particular wisdom your body has to offer.

Having a sensitive body type used to be a challenge for me. I thought it was a weakness. Self-acceptance became easier once I saw my sensitive nature as a gift and strength – an opportunity to enhance my empathic and intuitive abilities for healing, learning and loving connection.

Who you are - your essence, strengths and special traits - can be expressed in many ways. One way is through the physical body. Your body can reflect an *inner gift* or *message you have to share*. It can even give you clues about your life path. Be receptive; see your body as an ally and allow it to work for you and with you. Realize that your body has its own sacred way of being.

Plant seeds of self-care into your life so you can feel yourself grow and blossom.

Honoring and Loving Your Inner Body

Visualize your body in good health. Imagine and trust, that with each inhalation and exhalation, your breath calmly carries oxygen to every cell and organ, bringing daily renewal and relaxation to all your body systems.

When your body aches, feels unbalanced or sick, use loving self-talk and send it healing vibrations through visualization. Be patient and present. Listen for what your body needs. It might be asking you to slow down.

Choosing to eat plenty of healthy, whole foods and drinking fresh water on a regular basis will change the way your body feels, and over time will bring a radiant beauty from within. Reading or taking a class on body-mind connection and what a healthy relationship to food means is a good start for inner body self-care.

Loving your inner body means doing your best to feed it nourishing foods and liquids. Learning about nutrition or working with a nutritionist or counselor can help change your life. Your body and moods will become more balanced as you consume less alcohol, sugar, soda, caffeine, and deep-fried and packaged foods.

You are beautiful.

Honoring and Loving Your Outer Body

Wearing clothes, colors and accessories that inspire you and make you feel beautiful is an empowering expression of loving yourself and your body. Many cultures believe that body adornment reflects sacred, spiritual expression and connection with the Divine.

Physical appearance has the power to reflect how you are feeling inside, so dress yourself in alignment with how *you want* to feel, be and look. Embrace, express and celebrate your unique style to connect with who you really are.

When you move your body, you move your mind.

Moving and Praising Your Body

One of the forerunners of all self-care is body movement. It is the foundation - the base that makes all other self-care techniques and processes easier.

When I don't exercise, I have less energy, feel out of sync with myself and become tempted to forget the other important parts of my self-care routine.

The body is meant to move. When you move your body, you move your mind. Yoga, walking, biking, gardening, swimming, dancing and more are vital in supporting your self-care. Find a form of exercise that resonates with you, and do it. Praise yourself for doing it. Enjoy the results that come when you dedicate the time to exercise.

By simply moving your body in some way each day, you can make a positive and profound difference in your life.

In *spirit* creation

Expressing Your Creativity

Creative expression is a magical outlet. Express yourself through various forms - singing, writing, playing musical instruments, painting, sewing, dancing. We are creative 'energy beings' that can express ourselves in the most amazing, imaginative and inspiring ways. Enrich your self-care by diving into your true nature, which is to create.

Start simple. Doodle on note pads, plant a seed in a pot, sing in the shower, and make handmade gifts - anything to get your creative juices flowing. Relax and enjoy the art of creating, without judging yourself or attachment to the outcome.

Studies have shown that creativity increases upon completion of physical activity. After yoga, I often feel inspired to paint. Once I paint, I feel good about myself. I feel connected with a higher purpose and my sense of creative potential expands. I am 'in the zone.'

Establishing a flow-pattern of creativity:

For one month, set aside fifteen minutes each morning or evening to do something creative, like paint, drum, sing, dance or journal. After one month of these 'creative sessions', you will be surprised by how you feel and notice a difference in your flow of creativity. Keep it going.

Go easy. Be gentle. Self-nurture means being kind and compassionate with *you*.

Nurturing Yourself

Knowing how to nurture your own heart and emotional process when no one is available to give or share with you is a key component in self-care. Learning how to nurture yourself takes courage because there are times when others won't be able to nurture you when you need it most.

Emotions can be strong. But when you allow yourself to feel and accept your emotions, rather than be afraid of them, you build trust that *you* can take care of you. Getting into a practice of *experiencing* your feelings without judgment, and then letting them go, will lessen emotional overwhelm, negativity and attachment.

To authentically nurture myself, I had to learn self-compassion. Self-compassion is a soft stillness of the heart, a tender loving reverence for self. It is the desire and willingness to help, heal and understand the self.

A spiritual mentor once told me, "Love yourself up. Give yourself lots and lots of love and compassion. Fill yourself up. And then, from your overflow, give to others." Learn how to nurture yourself with compassion so that you may nurture others.

Things you can do to nurture your heart and soothe emotions:

1. Self-massage your entire body with an organic oil (jojoba, coconut, sesame or shea are nice.) Add several drops of your favorite organic essential oil for aromatherapy and relaxation. Lavender and rose essential oils have been known to calm and soothe emotions.

2. Listen to music that is soft and nourishing.

3. Give yourself gentle, loving reassurance when you feel down or vulnerable.

4. Receive foot reflexology, massage, cranial sacral, reiki or acupuncture. These kinds of modalities can help heal on a physical, emotional and soul level.

5. Make yourself a cup of tea or soup; take a warm bath or shower, curl in bed and rest.

6. Read something spiritual or uplifting.

7. Journal your thoughts and feelings.

8. Light candles, meditate, pray.

9. Make time to observe and tune in to the grace and beauty of nature and animals.

10. Lay in 'child pose', a resting pose.

Child pose: comforting and soothing: Kneel on the floor, dropping the buttocks toward your heels and sitting on your heels. Bring the knees hip width apart. With both palms on the ground, begin bending at the elbows and bowing down until your forehead rests on the ground. Use a folded blanket under your forehead for modification if it doesn't reach the ground. Your chest and stomach rest on, between or close to your thighs. Palms face down on the ground near or above your head. Relax your arms, shoulders and neck. For three minutes, rest comfortably and let go of any physical or emotional 'holdings' or stress.

<u>*Relaxing even deeper within yourself:*</u> After three minutes, begin rubbing your forehead on the ground (or blanket) in a circular motion, sideways and up and down, in the areas that need attention. Palms are still face down on the ground. Babies naturally do this in the crib upon awakening. Rubbing your forehead on the ground and especially the center, the 'third eye' area, helps stimulate the pituitary gland. Stimulating the pituitary gland is soothing and also activates the pineal gland. When these two glands work in unison, your nervous system harmonizes, allowing you to relax and become 'one' with yourself. In this state of comfort, more clarity is possible.

Self-care is not about comparison or judgment.
Find your own north star. Your star will look
different from another's.

Balancing and Harmonizing Your Mind

A healthy mental balance requires self-care too. Being heard is one of the most important things as a human being. Are you being heard? Surround yourself with people - work, friendships, and love relationships - that allow your mind and soul to feel free, honored and heard.

If you are someone who needs to communicate often in order to process your thoughts and emotions through conversation, consider a talk therapist or support group as part of your self-care.

Remember to be gentle with yourself, especially when dealing with stress, a broken heart, disappointment or loss. Words and thoughts are powerful. Listen to what you think and say. To calm and quiet your mind, talk to yourself with patience and love. Beating yourself up mentally because of a situation or a choice you made or a choice you aren't ready to make causes more unhappy feelings.

Creating loving and life-affirming beliefs and actions are crucial for mental balance. Having an open, encouraging mind-set helps keep negativity in check.

Meditation and yoga have helped me with this. *Yoga Nidra* is one style of meditation that brings mind-body relaxation and a profound sense of peace. *Kundalini Yoga* offers a plethora of meditations that can immediately shift energy and mind-set through chanting, music and mudras.

The best way to cultivate self-love is through self-care.

Self-Care and The Self-Love Connection

Self-care directly correlates with self-love. When you authentically love yourself, you want to care for yourself and see yourself 'succeed' emotionally, mentally, physically and spiritually. Sabotaging yourself and your life by making choices that are disempowering or ignoring your needs to please another means you aren't loving or valuing yourself. To embrace your fears and look deeper within yourself takes time and sometimes expert help from a mentor or spiritual counselor.

Discovering I didn't know how to love myself was heartbreaking, but I learned to accept it. Over time I was able to make changes by slowing down, inquiring within, and taking time to understand my fears. As I began to heal myself with forgiveness and these self-care steps and techniques, I learned to *feel* what loving myself meant.

Self-love is accepting your *existence* in this life with compassion and trust, just as you are now. Self-love is having the courage to discover who you are *without having to be or achieve anything* in order to be loved. Remember: there is no such thing as perfect!

"I AM" - Connecting with your heart and soul

Saying the words "I AM" with meaning and intent, is powerful. Repeating the words, "I AM" can harmonize and reaffirm the truth of your existence and oneness.

Sit in a chair with both feet flat on the floor. Sit tall, place both hands over your heart center and relax. Take your time. Breathe in deeply through your nose and out your mouth three full rounds. Keeping both hands on your heart, begin to breathe naturally, and focus on your heartbeat.

Close your eyes and concentrate on the third eye point, the center between your brows. Really feel the pulse of your heartbeat in your hands, relax your shoulders and your face. With the rise and fall of each breath, whisper seven times, "I AM." Then out loud, repeat "I AM" seven times.

ABUNDANCE
A Self-Care Poem

There is abundance for you child

There is enough

There is an abundance of food for you child

There is enough

There is an abundance of money for you child

There is enough

There is an abundance of love for you child

There is enough

There is an abundance of energy for you child

There is enough

You are enough

There is an abundance at all times for you

For all.

Do not go astray because you do not believe.

You can take care of yourself

You can do it.

Refill, refill and refill

Accept the abundance

You need not go anywhere to "get it"

It is here. Right now.

Take care of yourself

Give to yourself

Breathe

Receive

Abundance.

Self-Care Is

- Saying NO to someone so you can say YES to yourself
- Going to bed early when you need rest and renewal
- Going out when it's time for joy and celebration
- LISTENING to your own heartbeat
- Being in water: swimming, natural hot springs, a bath, ocean
- Eating whole, real foods, vegetables, fruits, seeds, nuts
- Treating yourself to your favorite chocolate or treat
- Making choices from LOVE rather than fear
- Being with friends and lovers who care for and inspire you
- Spending more time in nature - reading, drawing, dreaming
- Making healthy, honest, safe, sexual and sensual connections

- Expressing gratitude for who you are in this moment
- Focusing on your STRENGTHS rather than weaknesses
- Laughing, dancing, singing, crying
- BEING with animals
- Drinking pure clean water throughout your day
- Preparing healthy meals and desserts
- Writing down 3 things you love about YOURSELF each morning
- Surrounding yourself with your favorite flowers
- Praising yourself and others out loud
- Learning to feel what it means to truly RECEIVE
- Feeling rather than judging
- Confiding in and being supported by people you trust
- Creating a sacred alter in your room, home or creative space
- Walking barefoot on the earth

A Message For You

I have learned a great truth: that I can know myself and want to help myself, but real change only takes place when I have a desire, willingness and commitment to self-care. Some people feel they don't have the time or patience for it. Many feel it's 'too late' or they aren't worth it.

If you don't make the time now, when will you? If you aren't worth the time now, then when will you be? Self-care is a journey. A journey you can make anytime no matter what your past or present. *Come home* to yourself, to the spiritual wealth and love within, through self-care.

ACKNOWLEDGMENTS

Special thanks to my *purrfect* writing partner, Mr. P; my editor Alissa Lukara, for her expertise and encouragement; my partner David, for his grace and support; my father, for his healing wisdom and mentorship; my mother, for her loyalty and strength; my sister, for her insight and enthusiasm; Roger and Alexandra, for their great inspiration and friendship.

To work with Dena or to order additional copies of
Loving Who You Are, visit DenaLeighCarter.com

www.ingramcontent.com/pod-product-compliance
Lightning Source LLC
Chambersburg PA
CBHW031429290426
44110CB00011B/591